Rumbling into your home t attitude and badder grammar you into human gorgonzola ↑ pulp paperback dum-dui fourth issue of Men of

I am in the strange position of writing an editorial for issue 4 a couple of years after it was published! The original, in a good old-fashioned limited print run as opposed to the Createspace/Amazon print on demand version you currently hold in your hands, didn't have much of an editorial, and the illustration I ran won't fit in with the format of this reprint.

There are a couple of other additions to this reprint. One an article on the Headhunters which I've used to beef up this issue's contents and some capsule reviews for Lou Cameron books that never made it into issue four.

The Headhunters is a relatively unknown and under-appreciated series, which deserved to stick around for longer. Written by two journalists in Detroit, the first book opens with the preface - *"This is a work of fiction. It is dedicated to Detroit, America's meanest city. If the events depicted here haven't happened yet, they probably will. It's that kind of place."*

I drove through the outskirts of Detroit in 2016 and saw entire streets and neighbourhoods seemingly deserted and abandoned. I've never personally witnessed anything quite like it in terms of poverty.

When pulling together this reprint I did consider rewriting some of the articles, but came to the conclusion that I should just run them as they originally appeared without any revisions. So appalling punctuation and grammar appear as they originally did. And it wouldn't surprise me if I had inadvertently introduced a few more along the ways!

Whether I will feel the same way about presenting material from the first couple of issues without some serious rewriting, I really don't know. Those first two issues were especially crude, in every sense, my fanzine equivalent to those photos of you as an acne ridden, mullet sporting and gangly teenager that your parents excavated from a dusty corner and gleefully showed the first serious girlfriend took home (don't tell me that was only my parents?!?). I would probably rather those early efforts also stayed in the side-board.

But on second thoughts.....that mullet was pretty rockin' wasn't it?

thepaperbackfanatic@sky.com

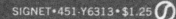

SIGNET•451-Y6313•$1.25

#5

THE REVENGER

JON MESSMANN

CITY FOR SALE

THE MAFIA HELD NEW YORK CAPTIVE ON A MURDER-GO-ROUND – UNTIL BEN MARTIN PUT A STOP TO A ROLLER COASTER OF DEATH.

"WHO OFFENDS, WRITES ON SAND; WHO IS OFFENDED, ON MARBLE."

Although ultimately the first of a series of six paperbacks, *The Revenger* (by Jon Messmann, Pyramid, 1973) was un-numbered, and its ending was far from open-ended, suggesting that either author Messmann or publisher Signet were testing the waters for such a character before entering the market. That the second entry didn't appear for a further nine months also indicates that Signet hadn't commissioned a block of books to release as a series.

Prior to tackling *The Revenger,* I wasn't sure which version of the author I would encounter. Was it the uninspired hack with dodgy sexual politics of Nick Carter adventure *The Casbah Killers* (1969)? Or was it the inventive hack with dodgy sexual politics of another Carter, the fast-paced Red Scare opus *Operation Che Guevara* (1969)?

In truth, it was a bit of both. But in addition, there was a sustained intensity and simmering tension in the narrative that I hadn't previously thought Messmann capable of, or paid enough to be sufficiently motivated to deliver. This tone was perfect for the book's subject matter and Messmann portrays the mind-set of the lone vigilante and his tactics better than any other men's adventure author, with the exception of Our Lord, Don Pendleton. (Say three 'Stay Hards' in absolution!)

Ben Martin is the titular character, a local business-owner in New York who objects to the Mafia extending their protection-racket to his neighbour-hood. When he intervenes in the beating of an elderly man refusing to pay protection, Martin is set on a collision course with the Mafia. It results in the death of his son, the collapse of his marriage and a self-destructive vendetta to wipe out the hoods responsible.

Messmann plays out the politics and mind-set of the lone-wolf perfectly, using the middle-class and liberal friends of Martin's wife as contrast to his un-bending world-view. Although Messmann uses Martin's wife to make the point that his refusal to compromise has cost them their son and their marriage, he is unequivocal in his portrayal of Martin regarding it as a more palatable cost than a betrayal of his principles.

"We're afraid the world will blow up in our faces someday. We're afraid and losing all the good things we have. People don't want to be afraid of anything else. They'd rather turn away from trouble."

"That's stupid. That's how to bring on trouble."

"Being afraid isn't a sin," Donna says quietly.

"I don't know about that," he answers. *"Maybe it is. Maybe it's the worst sin of all."*

The book is far from action-packed, but as a result, when the

violence does explode it is all the more hard-hitting. Such as when the local enforcers turn up to intimidate Martin, just after he has opened the morning post with a bayonet turned letter-opener. Have the goons never read one of these books?

Inside the gray-eyed man there is an explosion. First there is a kind of disbelief, and then a paroxysm of shattering, erupting outrage. Matty's words, and the presence of the two men, detonate all the seething sense of fury that is within Ben Martin. His hand closes around the hilt of the letter opener and in a motion too quick for the eye to follow, he slams the bayonet blade of it into the man's right hand, feeling the point tear through flesh and bone and plunge deep into the hard wood of the desk top under the hand. He hears the man's scream of pain over his own words. "You sonofabitches," he says. "You rotten, dirty, stinkin' bastards."

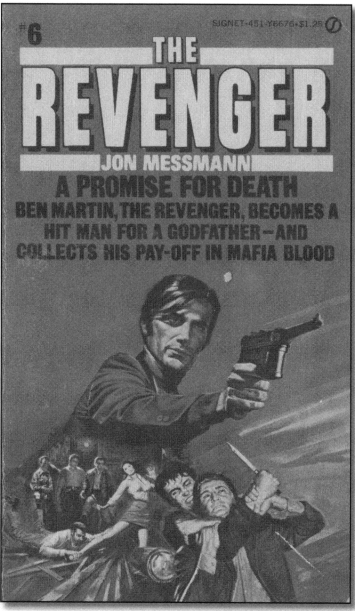

It transpires that Martin was a Special Forces operative, a sniper specialising in lone wolf missions in Vietnam, and he uses the very same tactics to wipe out the Mafia goons. In one breathlessly taut sequence, Martin embarks on a meticulously choreographed series of assassinations. No charging into the enemy's lair with blazing magnums for Martin, he uses a sniper scope from a distant roof-top to turn his enemy's heads into mush (imagine a Tom Savini special effect from *Maniac* or *Dawn of the Dead*), immediately dumps his weapons and escapes through a mapped-out route.

Ben fires again, only two shots again, perfectly aimed, dead on target. Two shots only. Never fire more than you need to fire. Never stay back to fire when you should be getting away. Matty's head gushes like a red geyser as he catapults to the sidewalk, and the second man falls half over him. They also make a crude cross as they lie there. Ben Martin does not see this, though. He is going down the other stairway and out of the building.

In another excellent scene seething with tension, Martin goes shopping for guns. A lengthy conversation takes place between the manager and Martin about distance, accuracy and calibre. I don't go for all that technically accurate gun porn so beloved by many men's adventure fanatics, but for me the kick is the reader being in on the true nature of Martin's prey.

The salesman, following along, watched the big man. "Big game this time, is it?" he ventured. The gray-eyed man lowered the rifle and nodded, still unsmiling.

Could Messmann maintain the intensity across the next five books? Inevitably the answer is no, with the sixth and final episode, *A Promise For Death* (1975) a very different book to the first and more in keeping with traditional imitators in the field. It's an ignoble start when an aspiring ballerina is raped by a gang of greasy street hoods and the story heads into over-familiar *Death Wish* territory. Martin is considered dead by the Mafia but as he is now working in the delivery business of the ballerina's father, decides to take on another mission. Retribution is delivered to the punks, but Martin is reckless and naive compared to the thoughtful

SIGNET • 451-Q6097 • 95¢

#4

THE **REVENGER**

JON MESSMANN

THE STILETTO SIGNATURE

SEX MINGLES WITH SAVAGERY AS BEN MARTIN, THE REVENGER, HUNTS DOWN THE KILL-CRAZY NEW OVERLORD OF THE MAFIA

and cold-blooded character of the first book.

Just as this reader guessed the story was heading in one direction and was beginning to fight an urge to flick through a few pages, Messmann flips it on its head by revealing the assault was arranged by cunning Mafia chief Aldo Trafficante to flush Martin out of hiding. Slapbang in the middle of an internal gang-war and with his own daughter kidnapped, Trafficante wants to employ Martin to wipe out his rivals.

From here on, Messmann deals out a number of twists and turns, which are not always ingenious but certainly are engaging. And Martin returns to his logical, ice-cool self when rescuing Trafficante's daughter from kidnappers or drawing out his rivals with a baited trap.

Cynical, violent and trotting along at a goodly pace, you can do a lot worse than check out this episode. I haven't read the other four **Revenger**s, but based on their back cover blurbs the most lurid and therefore interesting is *The Stiletto Signature* (October 1974) in which a new generation of younger and more brutal Mafioso is imported from Italy to run a nifty line in whiteslavery.

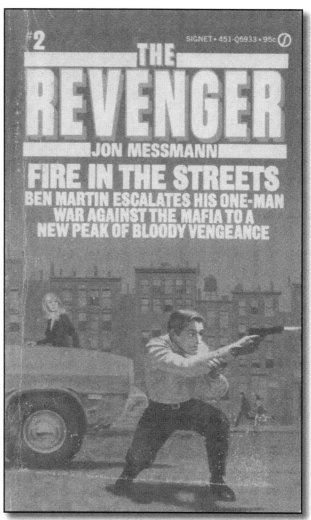

In summary, **The Revenger** series is a superior member of the army of **Executioner** clones from that period, with the first episode in particular, burning with an acetylene-torch style of writing that perfectly encapsulates the mind-set of pulp psychosis and the actions of a man who is military trained and doesn't care if he is convicted as long as he completes his mission of retribution. Step forward, Ben Martin, man of violence!

SCREW THE HATEFUL 8

A review of The Devil's Dozen, one of three Nick Carters written by Martin Cruz Smith

Prior to becoming famous for cold-war thrillers such as *Gorky Park*, Martin Cruz Smith was chipping away at the coal-face of men's adventure fiction with **The Inquisitor** series (as Simon Quinn at Dell) and three Carters, including *The Devil's Dozen (1973)*, which I'll review here.

I'm pleased to report this can be added to the pile of Smith must-reads in the men's adventure genre, as *The Devil's Dozen* achieves the juggling act of remaining faithful to the Carter formula whilst keeping the execution fresh and invigorating.

When a fellow AXE agent who has been investigating Mafia heroin smuggling is fatally poisoned, Carter is tasked with creating a method to bring all of the Mafia heads together in one place, so the agents of A.X.E. can swoop in and destroy them. Who needs a justice system with A.X.E. in town!?! Carter's approach is to pose as Riki Senevres, a Turkish smuggler who can provide unheralded amounts of high-grade heroin for distribution by the US based Mafia.

His plan succeeds and he is granted an audience with the titular 'devil's dozen' of Mafioso at a mountain-side retreat in Colorado, but faces two sources of trouble – his identity slipping under the scrutiny of the suspicious Mafioso, and the retreat's array of weaponry which will surely defeat any AXE troops.

Despite most authors undoubtedly treating a Carter as hack-work, Smith still brings plenty to the table. Carter's plan to smuggle the heroin is ingenious and explains the map of Europe included in the preface. Smith also mixes humour with violence to great effect, especially in one climatic scene.

"Every Mafioso in Snowman was waiting for me. In the middle was King. Next to King were the new arrivals: Charlie DeSantis and a Turk. The Turk stood around six foot seven and weighed 340 lbs. His neck was as large as most mens' thighs. His skull was shaved. His face was a scarred scowl, decorated with a mustache. If he'd pulled an arm off the nearest chief and eaten it as a late night snack I wouldn't have been amazed.

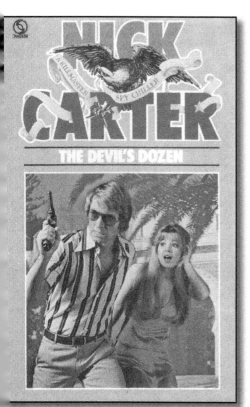

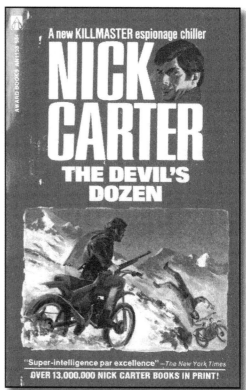

King didn't disappoint me, though.

"Raki Senevres, he addressed me, "I want you to meet Raki Senevres," and he patted the Turk on the back.

I was more than amazed."

It's the little touches that Smith brings which also make a difference, such as Carter's self-reflection that his make-up as Raki accentuates a certain cruelness to his face (I can't imagine many Carter hacks bringing that type of genuflection to their characterisation of the spy) or mentioning the symbols daubed on a horse-drawn cart in Bulgaria for protection against the evil-eye.

I must also call out Smith's portrayal of the lead female with whom Carter forms an uneasy alliance and is central to the book. Vera is the daughter of a Mafia don and sports a poisonous ring, making her chief suspect in the death of Carter's colleague. Smith pens Vera as sassy, resourceful and courageous, and despite her deadly potential, Carter finds himself deeply attracted to her (me too!). A long way from the kidnap-bait ciphers most ghost-writers featured in Carters.

Could Smith have kept up this quality if he had produced at the rate of say, a Ralph Hayes? I don't know, but *Devil's Dozen* is worth twelve run-of-the-mill Carters.

THE DESTROYERS
OPERATION IL DUCE
CHARLES WHITING

THE DIRTY HALF-DOZEN

A look at The Destroyers, a world war two adventure series from Charles Whiting.

In the 1970s and 80s, Whiting was a veritable one-man pulp army, producing tough and gritty world war two actioners to huge success in the UK, in particular with a series as Leo Kessler about Wotan, a crack German regiment.

Whiting was an ex-soldier and a military historian with a prodigious work ethic, with 250+ books to his name. Whiting was still writing, up until his death in 2007, at one point losing a leg in a mountaineering accident but carrying on his work from a hospital bed. His books were about as accurate as you could get in a genre which demanded a certain smattering of sex and violence, and he churned them out at an impressive rate.

Normally Whiting only his used his own name for his non-fiction, typically using pseudonyms for his disposable pulpier war fiction. Therefore it was unusual that **The Destroyer** series, which was written for Sphere Books in the UK, appeared as by Charles Whiting. He belted out all six titles in eighteen months - impressive enough without taking into account he was also producing work as Leo Kessler at a rival publisher.

The series was renamed **The Dirty Devils** in the USA when Pinnacle reprinted three from 1975 to 1977, with slightly revised titles. Pinnacle's re-titling of the series is undoubtedly to suggest *The Dirty Dozen*, which gives the best indication of their inspiration and tone.

Leader of The Destroyers is ruthless Lieutenant Crooke (geddit?) V.C., who sports a pirate style eye-patch. His crew of ex-cons include Gippo, the half-breed pimp; Stevens, the black marketer; Yank, the merciless Texan killer; the Guardsman, the ex-sergeant-major; and

Thaelmann, the hard-bitten German communist. Readers of the Sven Hassel books, which were even more popular in the UK (although he was nicknamed "Seven Arseholes" by some Kessler fans due to the far-fetched nature of his stories) will recognise some of the character types.

Whiting undoubtedly was a formula writer, and when your formula is as successful as his, you can't blame him for sticking to it. *Operation Kill Ike* is typical of the series, with Whiting employing a well-known military figure to provide an anchor-point of reality, in this case, an assassination plot against Eisenhower. A Whiting

speciality is to juxtapose historical quotes with those of his own creation, blurring the lines between the fact and fiction and a nifty short-cut to bringing a sheen of authenticity to his work.

Chapters are no longer than 6 pages, so the books are easy to pick up for a few minutes at a time. There is little to be found in suspense or character development, with Whiting employing clipped, crisp language to keep the plot hurtling forward at break-neck speed. The tone is cynical, almost know-it-all, with Whiting letting the readers in on the joke, which I imagine would be hugely appealing to those who shared his fascination for military detail and the workings of the Army. These books would have undoubtedly been enjoyed equally by soldiers as barrack reading, and by arm-chair warriors.

Although reviewers often mention sex and violence as a key element of Whiting's pulpier work, it does tend to be brief and is used to be propel the plot forward. The violence is deadly and often presented with a sardonic comment, but Whiting doesn't dwell in the detail, in the way the afore-mentioned Sven Hassel might do (I've always preferred Hassel!). His depiction of sex is transactional, and I would compare its use with a magician's sleight of hand; look over here at a strip show in the Pigalle whilst I slip in some lengthy dialogue as Crooke receives his mission briefing from a perspiring civil servant.

When I picked up **The Destroyers** I wanted to read the story depicted by the Pinnacle covers; dynamic, action-packed with brick-jawed heroes letting rip with machine-pistols whilst the air fills with explosions. What I got were the unglamorous, dirty and grim-faced stories depicted by the artist for the Sphere editions.

This series will undoubtedly appeal to those who want a stream-lined and quasi-believable series of world war two espionage pulps.

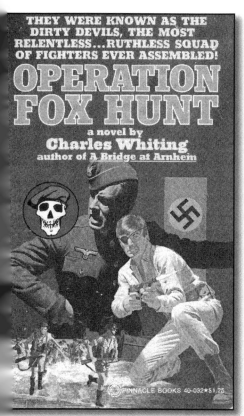

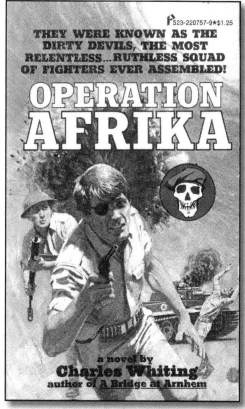

$2.25
BH082

RADCLIFF #1

TAKES A CONTRACT ON HARLEM'S
MOST CLOSELY GUARDED MAN

HARLEM HIT

by ROOSEVELT MALLORY

HIT-MAN

Holloway House, inventor of the 'Black experience' paperback, published four novels in the Radcliff series.

Holloway House started off as a run-of-the-mill sleaze publisher, with a catalogue consisting of salacious biographies of tinsel town starlets and adaptations of ribald movies. But by the late 60s had stumbled on a successful formula of publishing books at aimed at black Americans, or as Holloway called it, "the black experience". It may have been owned by two white men with a rather hit-and-miss approach to paying royalties, but Holloway debuted a number of important black writers such as Iceberg Slim and Donald Goines.

As you might expect, Holloway did try a few characters which could be considered black versions of the likes of **The Executioner** (in the grindhouse cinema tradition of *Blacula* and *Blackenstein*, any takers for **The Blax-ecutioner** anyone?); specifically **The Ice-Man** and **Radcliff**. I was expecting more in the genre, as pretty much every publisher sharing the lower rungs of the publishing ladder with Holloway were flooding the market. I wonder if the reason was if Holloways' distribution didn't particularly support ongoing series. Although **The Ice-Man** was the longer running of the series, with seven books to **Radcliff**'s four, it is the lesser of the series in my view, so I'll concentrate on Radcliff.

Radcliff lives in Florida in a super-fly pad, with running hot blondes on tap, a fuelled up Lear jet on-call, as well as an ex-army buddy who now invents weapons and explosive devices for him. Being Holloway House, they also replicated elements of **The Executioner**, such as him being a Vietnam veteran and battling the Mafia, but introduced differences they felt would appeal to their audience.

So they made Radcliff is a professional hit-man, using his Nam skills to earn his renegade living, identity unknown but his rep earning him the underworld nickname "Hit Master." Why they used **Radcliff** as the series title over **Hit Master**, which would have nicely encapsulated the series, I don't know. Maybe because Radcliff still sounds pretty cool and bad-ass.

Just to let the reader know that Radcliff isn't a Mack Bolan or a James Bond, the opening scene in first book, *Harlem Hit*, shows Radcliff assassinating a drug-lord. Not by shooting him from a distant roof-top through a sniper scope, but by strolling up to him and blasting him to bits with a shotgun, also peppering the lord's wife with pellets and traumatising their two young sons who are out for a walk with their parents. Unfortunately the book doesn't keep up this outrageous opening throughout the series, but the point has been made; this is the Holloway House equivalent to Janet Leigh's shower-scene in *Psycho* – all bets are off!

I assumed that Roosevelt Mallory was a pseudonym as the books are so cleanly written and therefore written by an experienced writer-for-hire. Checking the copyright records shows the books were actually copyrighted to Mallory, and whilst this is not infallible proof of the existence of an author, I also found an on-line

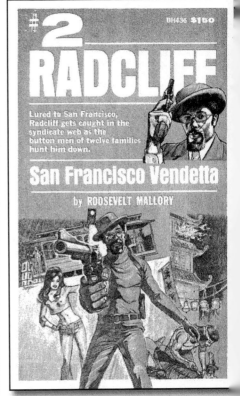

article profiling Mallory. It was in **Insider**, Hewlett Packard's in-house company magazine! Here's what it said about Mallory-

"Today, he's a TV director in the Data Systems training department, and previously served the division as a computer instructor.

He came to the career in a way familiar to many black people: the hard way. It began on an Alabama share-cropping farm, followed by years in a Birmingham ghetto. There, the everyday violence encouraged Mallory, a top student and athlete, to drop out and enlist in the army. This in turn led to some college work and the Coast Guard where he became an electronics technician, then instructor in electronics. After discharge he trained as a computer instructor, arriving at HP in 1966 where he became the company's first professional computer instructor.

Joe Radcliff got his start after Mallory had seen

one of the early hit-man movies featuring a black hero. "It didn't hang together," he says, "There were all these tough things going on – but no continuity. Bad writing! I knew I could write a believable script, so on evenings and weekends I dashed off the first draft of *Harlem Hit*. I also took a course in how to sell a script,

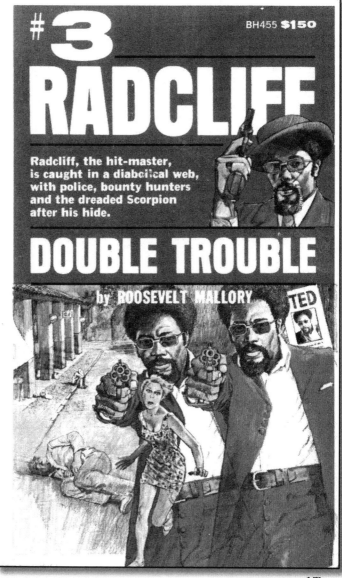

#**3**

BH455 **$150**

RADCLIFF

Radcliff, the hit-master, is caught in a diabolical web, with police, bounty hunters and the dreaded Scorpion after his hide.

DOUBLE TROUBLE

by ROOSEVELT MALLORY

which led me to my publisher. He liked the story, but asked me to rewrite the ending so that Radcliff survived. That way we could develop a Radcliff series."

"Of course, Radcliff is really working for Mallory. Some 50,000 copies of *Harlem Hit* have been sold, a second book titled *San Francisco Vendetta* is due out, and a third is still in the type-writer. The earnings and advances from those have enabled Mallory to expand his life style somewhat along the lines of the hit master – at least in such material manifestations as custom clothes and favoured wines. However, his real-life haunts are unlikely settings for a man who writes about violence: with his family; on a salmon fishing boat off the Golden Gate; a trout stream in the Sierra; some golf or skiing if his old football injuries permit.

The hit master, who makes his hideaway in the green depths of the Santa Cruz mountains would probably dig that – given the chance."

This pen-portrait of Mallory helped bring some insight to some of the elements of Radcliff book one, *Harlem Hit,* in which Radcliff is hired by the Mafia to assassinate Leroy Johnston, a radical politician who has been driving all of the drug

dealers, and therefore the Mafia's profit, out of Harlem. No white man would get close to Johnston or by his giant body-guard Llumba (I pronounce it 'lumber'!) so the Mafia turn to Radcliff who is an equal opportunities killer-for-hire, with a plan to double-cross him when the job is done, absolving them of any blame.

It is very plot-driven, with the excitement generated by the number of twists and break-neck pace rather than any great involvement in the characters. This feel very much is in keeping with

the book's origin as a film script. The title of the magazine piece was 'Get Mallory!' which was likely to be a reference to *Get Carter* the classic British book and film. What is not so well known is that the film received a remake as part of the soul-ploitation genre, as *Hit Man (1972)*. That Mallory includes a thread of sexual tension between Radcliff and his frustrated land-lady in *Harlem Hit*, and references a hit-man film in his article is a good indicator that was his inspiration.

I would describe Mallory's stripped-down, bare bones narrative style as "McCurtinesque", after the legendary editor and writer at Belmont Tower who oversaw so many of the men's adventure series of that period. Action-wise, it stays small-scale and gritty, with Radcliff fighting dirty and spending as much time fleeing through fire-exits with bullets flying through his hair as he does bursting in through doors with all guns blazing.

The continuity started in *Harlem Hit* continues throughout the mini-series, with Llumba returning in *San Francisco Vendetta*, the second book, as well the Mafia thirsting for vengeance after the damage inflicted by Radcliff. In *Double Trouble*, the action moves to Los Angeles, where the Mafia employ a double of Radcliff to create a trail of death. The fourth book was *New Jersey Showdown*, which I haven't read, but suggest the series was follow-

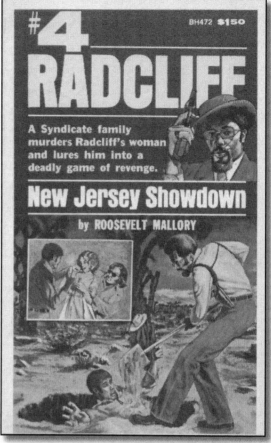

BH472 $1.50

#4 RADCLIFF

A Syndicate family murders Radcliff's woman and lures him into a deadly game of revenge.

New Jersey Showdown

by ROOSEVELT MALLORY

ing the pattern of the early **Executioners** which used cities in their titles, presumably as a sales boost in that locale.

(Holloway reprinted the series in the 1980s with new cover paintings by Corey Wolfe, but evidently missed up the covers, with *San Francisco Vendetta* showing a very clear sky-line of New York and a sewer tunnel which features in the climax of *Harlem Hit*.)

Looking at the author photo on the back of the books and in Hewlett Packard staff magazine, the cover artist on the first printings of Radcliff based the hit-man facial features on the author's.

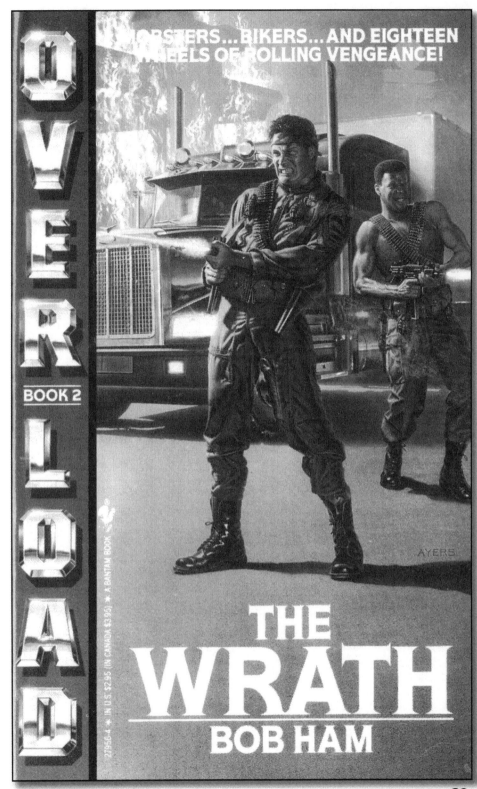

MOBSTERS...BIKERS...AND EIGHTEEN WHEELS OF ROLLING VENGEANCE!

OVERLOAD

BOOK 2

27956-4 ★ IN U.S. $2.95 (IN CANADA $3.95) ★ A BANTAM BOOK

AYERS

THE
WRATH
BOB HAM

OVERLOAD

It looks like Bantam made a concerted effort to break into the men's adventure market in the late 1980s, with three new series in the form of Dan Schmidt's Eagle Force (9 books, July 89 to May 91), Book of Justice by Jack Arnett (4 books, October 1989 to July 1990) and Overload by Bob Ham (12 books, June 1989 to September 1991). I take a perverse glee that the longest lasting was the latter, a 'trucker' series which seems such an un-commercial theme at first glance.

However, I do wonder if it was a smart move on the part of Bantam, as presumably truck drivers, away from home for long periods of time would be looking for reading material and the theme would naturally appeal to them. Bantam were very much marketing the series at truckers, even running instalments of the first book in **Overdrive**, a magazine aimed at truckers and published out of Tuscaloosa, Alabama. Based on the on-line examples I researched, the photo covers of **Overdrive** pandered to the hitchhiker-as-nympho fantasy of many a horn-dog trucker.

Certainly in the **Overload** series, the trucking theme is merely window-dressing, as much of the plot and resultant action could be lifted and dropped into any men's adventure novel. Its central two characters are Marc Lee and Carl Browne, a pair of Special Forces commandoes who return to Marc's home-town on leave to find his father's trucking company infiltrated by the Mafia. When Lee and Browne take a heavy-handed approach to the situation, the Mafia respond by blowing up his mum and putting his dad in a coma. At that point it becomes the titular *Personal War* of the first entry to the series.

I have no clue as to the identity of author Bob Ham. That 13 books under the Ham name appeared in two years and nowhere else, plus the nature of the genre, points to it being a pseudonym, despite a lengthy "meet the author" section at the end of the book. Whomever he may have been, Ham provides the target audience exactly what they crave – square-jawed heroes, colourful Mafioso, action set-pieces and greater attention to hardware accuracy than character development.

What did catch me by surprise was the level of sadism in the books. When Lee and Browne overpower a team of hoods they decide to teach them a lesson they won't forget; by severing their Achilles tendons with wire-cutters! My toes are curling just at the thought as I type it! At one point Browne shoves a revolver into the back passage of a prisoner as torture, and when he doesn't get the answers he wants, pulls the trigger. Compared to cold-blooded psychosis of the lead 'heroes', Segalini, the Mafia Don who uses the trucking company of Lee Senior for drug smuggling, seems noble and understandable.

There is an unheralded amount of violence to penises in *Personal War*. At one point a shot mafia goon shouts out "My god! The bastard shot my dick off!" and when Segalini tortures a captive Browne (for crippling his son with the Achilles treatment) with electric shocks, he enquires "Have you had enough, Mr Browne, or would you like me to see if I can make your dick explode with the next round?" Maybe Ham was tapping into deep-rooted fears? Other cultural archivists have commented on the close relationship between Lee and Browne, the two leads....

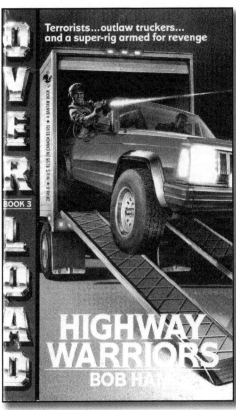

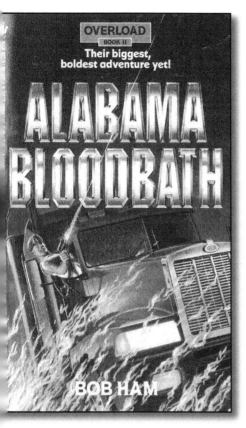

Where Ham displays strengths as a writer is in the extended chase sequence in which a desperate Browne flees into snow covered hills, hotly pursued by the Mafia in helicopters and on snow-mobiles who corner him in a mountain-side cave. Genuinely exciting and tense, Ham brings a cinematic feel to the sequence, and for a few chapters made me forget what a worthless psycho Browne was. The adventure ends in suitably dramatic fashion, with Lee confronting Segalini in a fiery inferno that is consuming his drugs factory and mansion.

Future books switched their theme between Lee and Brown mafia-busting (Segalini Junior survived the flames and returns in Book Two, *The Wrath*) and preventing terrorists from hijacking nuclear weapons from trucks. Some of the later entries also adopted the **Executioner** motif of including a location in their titles, such as *Alabama Bloodbath* and *Atlanta Burn*, but this was an intermittent tactic.

Although it may strike as a contradictory statement, I did enjoy large chunks of *Personal War* without wanting to ever read any more. So apologies to Tom Tesarek and Scott Carlson who literally drove hundreds of miles searching for entries to this series and dispatching them transatlantic to MoV HQ. True road warriors!

THE STEW-ART DOSSIER

In the previous issue I reviewed a Nick Carter by Valerie Moolman, noting it was a rare example of 'men's adventure' fiction penned by a female. Linda Stewart joins that select club, with two Carters to her name; *The Peking Dossier* (1973) and *The Jerusalem File* (1975). I enjoyed some brief correspondence with Linda by e-mail in 2015, and asked how she ended up writing the adventures of the super-spy.

"Right out of college, I'd written lyrics and sketches for nightclubs and off-Broadway, which, based on a good review in Variety, led to an ad exec offering me a job as a copywriter. I took it and kept it. It was still what's perhaps ironically called 'The Golden Age of Advertising', so I got to write a lot of 'hip' jingles and funny commercials in addition to the more serious stuff. At the same time, some close friends who had heavy celebrity clout were starting a monthly publication (straight journalism) and asked me to be the editor/main writer. The publication itself got a lot of publicity--we got to do guest shots on television--which led to my being asked to write articles for other magazines and led to my acquiring an agent at William Morris."

"Right off the bat, he got me a spot doing an episode for a shlock Sci-Fi series and, full of bravado, I decided to quit my day job, figuring I could always get another job in a year or so if I flopped. (There was also a healthy job market back then and, besides, I was still doing freelance journalism and freelance advertising so the rent would somehow get paid no matter what.)"

"His next inspiration came as a surprise."

A KILLMASTER SPY CHILLER

NICK ☆ CARTER ☆

THE PEKING DOSSIER

"For all the kinds of writing I'd done, I'd never written a word of prose fiction (nothing that required a "he said" after the dialogue) but he phoned me one day and asked if I'd ever read crime fiction. In fact, it was my favourite genre (Chandler, John D. MacDonald etc) and when I said so he told me the Carter series (which I'd never read) was looking for ideas and if I could come up with one and write a 35 page sample, he'd submit it. And so, with the naive nothing-to-lose chutzpah of the novice, I did."

"I'd just read an article in **Time Magazine** about the very first experiments in cloning, spun a plot around the idea, wrote 35 pages at the end of which I said, "this is how I think it ends and I have no idea what happens in the middle" and... It sold! (No one could get away with that today, which goes back to how relatively easy it was then.) I'm also pretty sure that those first 35 sample pages (except for the two opening lines) are pretty much, verbatim

and untouched, the first pages of *The Peking Dossier* as published."

Carter's mission in *The Peking Dossier* is to halt the mission of a Communist collective with the wonderful moniker of KAN (short for Kill Americans Now). The pesky Reds have discovered cloning technology, and as a result multiple copies of their master

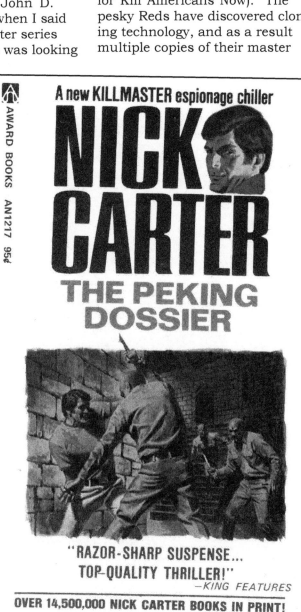

AWARD BOOKS AN1217 95¢

A new KILLMASTER espionage chiller

NICK CARTER

THE PEKING DOSSIER

"RAZOR-SHARP SUSPENSE... TOP-QUALITY THRILLER!"
—KING FEATURES

OVER 14,500,000 NICK CARTER BOOKS IN PRINT!

assassin are busy offing various senators to topple the American government. Kan (sorry!) Carter save the day?

Stewart is definitely a witty and sharp writer, and her version of Carter is the most humorous of any I've encountered, but for me she doesn't quite nail the character or the required tone. The book was published in 1973, but to my mind felt more in keeping the sexy-spy paperbacks issued by Lancer from the previous decade, where the unremittingly sassy style and sharp dialogue would have been much better suited.

"I ducked back into the girl's room, and stationed myself behind the door.

The door opened.

The girl gulped.

The godamn goon was so eager, he had his fly open before he closed the door. My mother told me to kick if I ever saw a rapist. I leapt from behind and got him by the throat. He clawed at my arms, but I spun him around. I got him back against the wall. I kicked.

Mother knows best.

He screamed. A blood curdler. Downstairs, they laughed. Those sadists thought it was the girl who'd screamed."

I don't think Stewart had worked out in her own mind whether Carter is a blue-eyed dream-boat or a psychotic. She was un-

doubtedly channelling the Sean Connery version of Bond in the plentiful romance sequences, but then switches Carter into terminate-with-extreme-prejudice killbot in the bat of an eye-lash. It was a bit too jarring for me. With the romance elements very much more front-and-centre, and with our lothario being the one who is ditched in a welcome reversal of roles, this is a very different take on Carter and I wondered what type of editorial input and/or interference Linda had received.

"Basically, none. I must have at some point been given a few existing Carters to read so that I understood about the organization he worked for and facts like that, but I pretty much established my own version of Nick in my 35 pages. I think, to make a character credible, he (or she) has to be YOUR character so I didn't worry about trying to be a copycat. I had no guidance while I was writing it, simply wrote it, turned it in. The editor assigned to Peking was the wonderful Agnes Birnbaum (now a literary agent) -- wonderful in that she liked what I was doing, trusted me, and left me and my plot, structure and prose alone, though here and there (rarely) she did add a line or two of what I considered over-explanation. These appeared in the published book."

"Even though this was my first stab at fiction, I just wrote the way I always write, which I guess naturally involves "care and dedication." I wrote in my own style and with my own take on the world --as it is and, more important for this kind of story, as it should be in mystery/adventure fiction-- and certainly with a deep involvement in the world I'm creating. I always worry about plot, about maintaining an internal as well as external logic, and worked hard to do that here."

of research into Middle East politics, places, customs, trying to make it a serious, though still snappy, thriller. But alas, while I was writing it Agnes left Award Books and another editor (who shall, to protect the guilty, remain nameless) had taken her place. After I turned it in, I never heard a word from her and never saw galleys or knew what she'd done to my book until I received the as-published copy. She had so thoroughly rewritten and clunked up the prose on almost every page, inserted her own lines, occasionally misunderstood my meaning and incorrectly reinterpreted it, that I was really heartbroken as well as angry and would never work for them again."

Stewart produced one other Carter, *The Jerusalem File* (1975), which I found a surprise when comparing her professional and polished work by some of the standards of hack-work from other authors Award were prepared to tolerate. Surely there must have been a reason why Linda didn't produce more Carters.

"I loved the manuscript of *The Jerusalem File* and I'd done a lot

After this bad experience, Stewart then specialised in movie tie-ins under the gender neutral pseudonym of Sam Stewart, such as *Harry and Walter go to New York* (Dell, 1976), *McCoy* and *McCoy: The Big Rip-off* (both TV, Dell, 1976), *Fun With Dick and Jane* (Dell, 1977), Ruby (Berkley 1978 as Kerry Stuart), *The Concorde Airport* (as Kerry Stuart, Jove, 1979). Of most interest to **MoV** readers is probably her tie-in to *Jackson County Jail* (Dell, 1977) the cult movie for which her then husband, Donald Stewart wrote the script.

I'm sure there were other works using pseudonyms, but Linda politely declined to provide any further details. Work appearing under her own name, received hard and soft-cover editions, and praise in the **NY** and **LA Times**.

Although I don't quite buy-in to Linda's vision of Nick Carter, I do wish her association with the character had been longer-lived. I admire how razor-sharp her writing was, and it was refreshing to read such a different slant on the character. There's no doubting she demonstrated a much greater level of creative flair and pride than many other contributors to the long-running series.

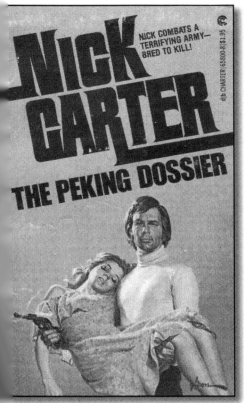

DETROIT MURDER CITY

A review of Quadrophonic Homicide, the fourth and final entry to The Headhunters series

The Headhunters' quadrology kicked off with *Heroin Triple Cross* (1974) then moved on to *Starlight Motel Incident* (1974) and *Three Faces of Death* (1974) before climaxing in *Quadraphonic Homicide* (1975). I'll focus on the latter in this appreciation of an excellent series.

Tough and gritty, the books are an effective melding of police-procedural with the hyper-sex and violence of the men's adventure genre-although the heroes are more likely to take evasive action when confronted by gun-wielding goons than engage in a head-long charge. In the world of The Headhunters, the heroes definitely aren't bullet-proof!

The Headhunters are Eddie Martin and T S Putnam, the former a snappily dressed hard-man, the latter a street-smart wise-cracker. Although laid-low by illness in *Quadraphonic Homicide*, their nemesis Henry Paquette instructs his henchmen to expand their drug trade from Detroit (the setting of the first two books) to Los Angeles. Uber-villains Mr Dust and Ton Ton Macquete delight in slicing and dicing their way through the movers and shakers of the LA record industry to gain control of the coke business. When Martin and Putnam connect the murder of a rookie cop with Paquette's mob they follow the bloody trail all the way to LA for a taste of Californian sunshine and slaughter.

Although I enjoyed the "odd couple" dynamic of Martin and Putnam, for me *Quadraphonic Homicide* is at its most entertaining when parading its colourful array of bad-guys. Quite literally in the form of Mr Dust who wears a lime-green sport suit, drives a lime-green Cadillac and wields a lime-green switch-blade. The fragrant and deadly "Mus-

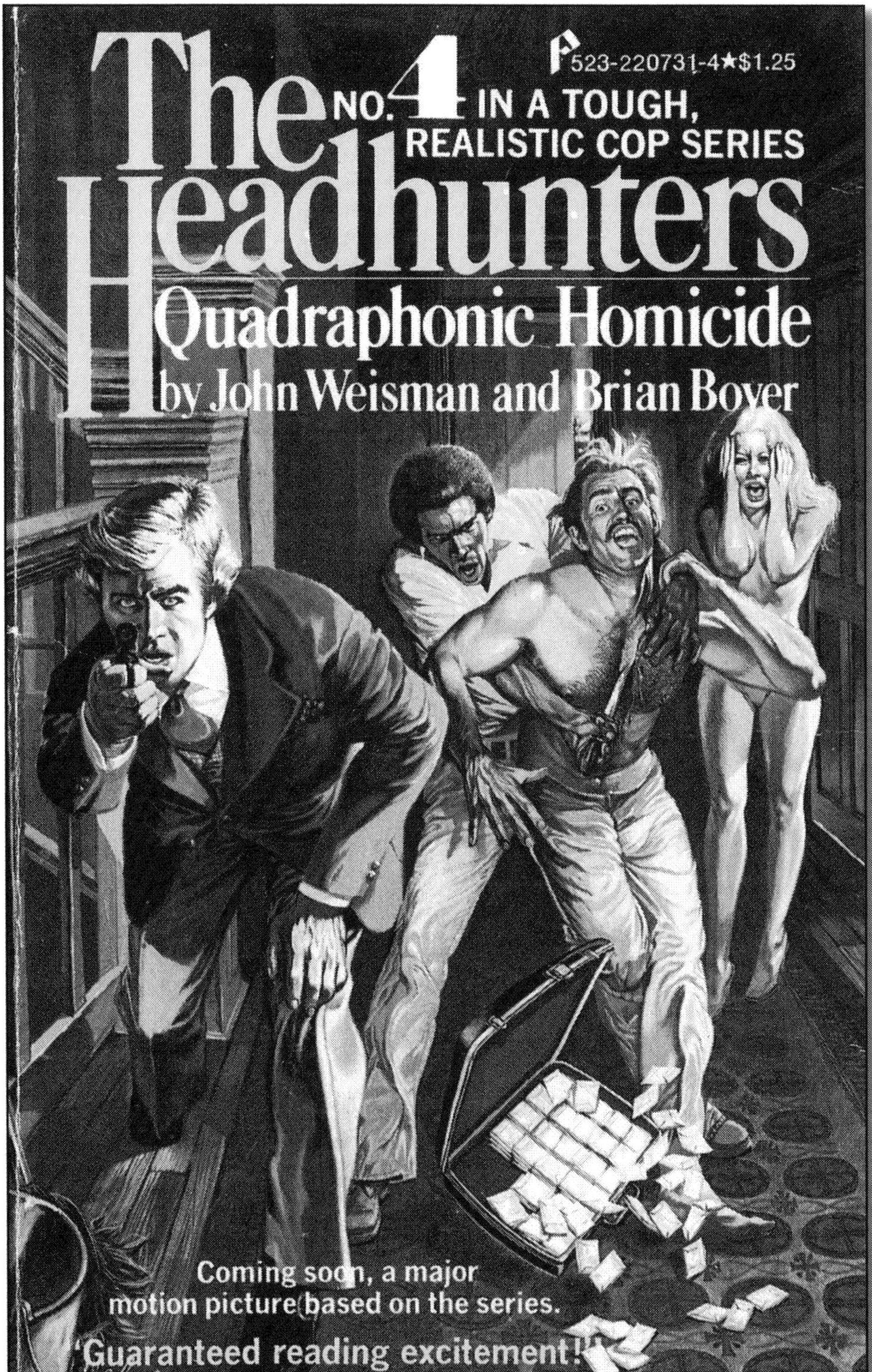
523-220731-4★$1.25
The Headhunters
NO. 4 IN A TOUGH, REALISTIC COP SERIES
Quadraphonic Homicide
by John Weisman and Brian Boyer
Coming soon, a major motion picture based on the series.
"Guaranteed reading excitement!" —Robin Moore

cles Mitchell" is the Pig Pen character from Peanuts all grown up into a total weapons-nut. And most memorable of all is the giant Haitian Ton Ton Macoute, a psychotic power-house with a taste for human eyeballs, who at one point takes on a great white shark and prevails!

At times the sex and violence does go beyond the realms of good bad-taste, specifically dialogue in which Macoute threatens to rape and eat someone's baby which made me feel very uneasy, but as co-author Weisman pointed out to me when I caught up with him for a chat about the series, their mentality when writing the books was to be as outrageous as possible. There's no doubting they succeeded on many levels.

When I asked if the pair were commissioned to produce an Executioner-clone he replied the literary inspiration for the series didn't come from Mack Bolan but another famous anti-hero; Travis McGee, who over 21 cult novels from the prolific John D McDonald, operated outside of the law as a "salvage consultant" charging 50% of the value of the goods (or person!) he was employed to recover.

Financial inspiration was provided by colleagues at the **Detroit Free Press** where the pair worked respectively as City Editor and Editor of "drugs and rock 'n roll." In 1973 during an after-hours drinking session at The London Chophouse, a bar the reporters would frequent, they took on a

$20 wager that they couldn't write a novel in seven days and then sell it. I would imagine that the challenge kick-started Boyer and Weisman into action on a previously discussed idea as opposed to $20 being sufficient motivation to become authors!

Further inspiration for the books was provided by the day-job and relatives. At one point Weisman had operated under-cover whilst investigating a case for the paper and his foster-brother had spent a couple of years working as an undercover cop in New York.

Certainly the first two books were all based on incidents reported in the **Free Press** during their tenure. A Detroit police captain who having been appointed in a wave of good publicity would eventually be imprisoned for corruption and drug-dealing provided the role-model for Henry Paquette, the heroin kingpin who would be the series recurring villain. And a real-life incident where police and sheriff's deputies had a fatal shoot-out with one another, with each side subsequently claiming they thought the others were drug-dealers (maybe more than a grain of truth in that one!) also provided the plot of book two *Starlight Motel Incident.*

Quadraphonic Homicide carries an air of authenticity in terms of how it describes the machinations of organised crime and in snatches of dialogue- think Dashiell Hammett hanging on 42nd street with a bad toot-habit!

The Headhunters

NO. **3** IN A DYNAMITE NEW SERIES

Three Faces of Death
by John Weisman and Brian Boyer

523-220432-9

"Guaranteed
reading excitement!"
—Robin Moore

"*We got cocaine, procaine, and blo-caine to do your do. Junk, Jones, horse, shit, and snow. We got marijuana, hashish, opium, morphine, LSD, THC, STP, DMT-sheeit, we even got FBI and CIA. We got yellows, reds, green-an'-blacks. We got laughers, criers, screamers, talkers. We got uppers, downers and middle-of-the-roaders. Then, we got some serious drugs.*"

Weisman told me he and Boyer would take turns visiting one another's house on the weekends (3 weekends of 8 hour days to write each of the books, resulting in an impressive production of 4 books in 24 days!) where they would alternate one being sat at the type-writer with the other shoulder-surfing and making suggestions. There was no particular type of scene one would specialise in and Weisman recalled that he could be at the type-writer, stop mid-way through a sentence of dialogue to go out to the kitchen and make a fresh cup of coffee, and by the time he got back to the seat Boyer would have completed the dialogue exactly how Weisman would have done it!

I love the image of two hard-bitten reporters locking themselves in a room, surrounded by clouds of smoke and mugs of steaming industrial-strength coffee, going at it hammer and tong in hacking out these books. As Weisman

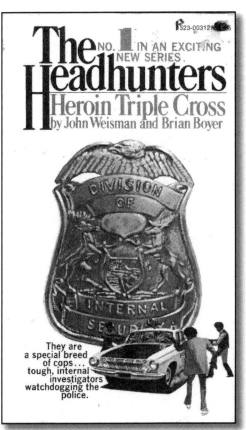

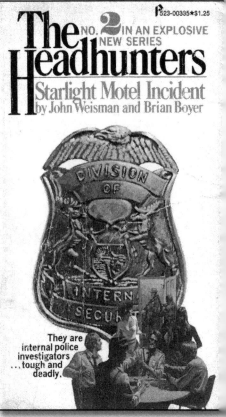

pointed out to me they were very much written in the first draft with little refining as both knew their readers were looking not for Pulitzer prize style dialogue but plenty of high-octane action.

Having completed the first book in six days, the pair sent it to New York based Robin Moore (probably best known as writer of *The French Connection*) who recommended it to Andy Ettinger at Pinnacle who offered a 3 book contract. After the first two books were written and set in Detroit, Weisman moved to a new job in Philadelphia and Boyer took up a post at the **Chicago Sun Times**. Their collaboration continued on the next two books, taking turns to fly out to one another's homes on a Friday night where they would then work over the weekend.

There's a lot of fun to be had in spotting the in-jokes and the pair's use of their friends in the books. Take for instance one particularly memorable scene in which Ton Ton cleaves the head of a great white shark in two with a machete. It's preceded by this dialogue referring to the shark's diet- "The destroyed police transmitter fell into its gullet where it lay indigestible alongside a gold signet ring bearing the crest of the Benchley family once swallowed off the coast of East Hampton." I guessed this was a reference to Peter Benchley who was scoring a mega-hit with *Jaws* at the time, but it wasn't until chatting to Weisman he revealed he had attended Princeton

with Benchley and was still in regular contact with the family.

The in-joke that inspired me to find out a bit more about this series was the use of a film producer character called Arthur Marks (The Headhunters use his boat) and the cover proclamation "Coming soon, a major motion picture based on the series." Marks was indeed a director and producer, probably best remembered for *Detroit 9000* a gritty exploitation film originally released in 1973 and given a limited cinema re-run a decade back when it was championed by Quentin Tarantino.

Marks was looking for a Detroit based follow-up and asked the pair to produce a film treatment and script which combined the first two Headhunter books. He also asked Weisman to devise a new Shaft-style blaxploitation hero, which Weisman obliged with a treatment called *Mr Chicago*, putting his regular visits to the Windy City to good use. At one point Marks flew Weisman down to New Orleans to work with Lou Gossett on dialogue for a forthcoming film, which I would guess was *J D's Revenge* a well-regarded blaxploitation horror number released in 1976.

Alas The Headhunters film never made it to the big screen, American International Pictures who released the majority of Marks pictures had enjoyed great success with exploitation films but from the mid-70s attempted to move into mainstream fare. It was a catastrophic move and AIP were out of business by the end of the decade.

When chatting to Weisman I mentioned that if I had done a bit more research prior to dropping him a line I wasn't sure if I would have had the guts to do it; Weisman is now an award-winning author of both fiction and non-fiction, and his site was plastered with photos of him with the founders of the US elite force Navy SEALS. Real-deal men of violence! And here I was ringing up over his breakfast to ask trivia about books he had written 35 years ago!

Weisman mentioned that he had lost contact with is ex-writing partner about twenty years ago, and that he suspected that Boyer dropped out of journalism around that time. Call me a sentimental old fool but this seemed a shame as the pair evidently had an effective working relationship with egos left by the door. They even flipped a coin to decide who was listed first on the cover.

I was pleasantly surprised as how open and accommodating Weisman was, and I think I only scratched the surface of his experiences during our twenty-minute call. I got the impression he was a matter-of-fact kind of guy with no airs or graces, with fond memories of these four books which served as a training ground for his journey from journalist to award winning author.

MORE GUTS THAN THE DIRTY DOZEN!

A review of three of Lou Cameron's early paperbacks

Lou Cameron (1924 – 2010) was an incredibly prolific creator in the disposable pulp market, initially starting as an artist in the vibrant comics industry where he worked for Atlas (the predecessor to Marvel) and DC, as well Classics Illustrated. In the 1960s he concentrated on the paperback market, initially on movie tie-ins, then thrillers, seeing out the late 70s and 1980s creating commercially successful adult western series such as Long Arm, Slocum and my personal favourite, Renegade.

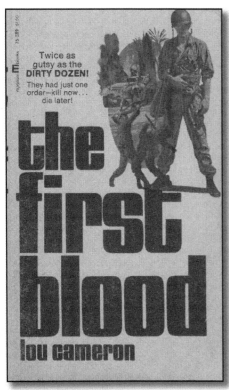

I decided to sample a trio of Cameron's 1970s paperbacks which didn't fall into the western genre, picking a pair of tough-cop thrillers and a world war two actioner. *The First Blood* (Magnum Books US, 1971) bought to mind **The Destroyers** series by Charles Whiting (see **Mov** 4), with a core of authenticity running through the two-fisted *Dirty Dozen* style premise. Anyone looking for a fast-paced, gritty and cynical world war two wham-banger will be well satisfied by this 160-page outing.

If war is defined as confusion, and Generals have to make decisions about soldier's lives made on a "bigger picture" basis, then Cameron nails it bang on in *The First Blood*. A group of marines are parachuted into Africa to protect a strategically vital fort which is threatened by a German tank division. With soldiers deserting, allegiances changing and mistakes made in the smoke and explosions of battle, *First Blood* successfully conjures up a bewildering experience that is also tremendously exciting. At times the writing can be confusing, with Cameron switching between using a character's real name and their nickname, but on the whole it works well.

Lt, Sean Fitzgerald is set up as the hero of the book, the leader of the mission and brave as a lion, but half-way through the book, Cameron delivers one of his typical curve balls – spoiler ahead – revealing him to be a crazed pill-popper who runs headlong into a hail of bullets, with fatal consequences. The character that then picks up the metaphorical reins is Roy Marvin, a huge machine-gunner who carries it about, suggesting this was an early prototype of the successful Renegade character.

Much of Cameron's earliest works were in the war fiction canon, with one of his earliest, *The Bastard's Name is War* (Gold Medal, 1963) a masterful combination of real events coated in hard-edged fiction. It even drew the attention of Harlan Ellison, who described Cameron as "a hell of a writer, one of the gutsiest writers on the scene. If this bombshell of a book doesn't make you grit your teeth, when you're not bawling or laughing, then you've wasted the price of the action: you ought to be reading Peter Rabbit."

Code Seven (1977, Berkley Medallion) is a titular reference to police slang for being off-duty, if indeed they can ever be off-duty, and Cameron's unsuccessful attempt to provide a gritty tough-copper. I would imagine this book was commissioned following the success of *The Choirboys* (1975) by Joseph Wambaugh, in which the author drew on his own experiences, as well as patrol-room legend, to produce a darkly humorous and hard-hitting account of how police privately cope with their professional lives. Based on Cameron's successful portrayal of barracks room humour and the camaraderie of the army in the likes of *The First Blood* and The

Renegade series, I had high hopes on this basis, but this was the most disappointing of the three I read.

Costello, one name only, is a straight-backed cop shifted to sleepy Florida beach-town following a run-in with the Mafia. But it doesn't take much digging to discover a cocaine smuggling operation and be plagued with suicide jumpers and trigger-happy robbers. So much opportunity for profanity, humour and shocks, but Cameron walks past all of them to provide a procedural thriller where the crimes are interlinked.

It's typical Cameron in that the plot unwinds at a leisurely pace and contains a cracking twist, but the characters are insufficiently developed and there is a lack of action to keep the pages turning. A real dud, a word I never thought I would use to describe a Cameron book.

Barca (1974) has a great pulp premise, in that the lead character is investigating his own potential murder as he is carrying an assassin's bullet is his brain which is inoperable but could move at any minute with fatal consequences. Very reminiscent of film noir classic *D.O.A.* (1950) in its premise, it has damn sight more energy to it than *Code Seven*, but, weighing in at 256 pages, it is as bloated as a week-old body fished from the river. You might still want to check this out as the UK edition carries several favourable write-ups from the likes of **Publishers Weekly**.

For now I'll be sticking with the tried and tested Renegade series from Cameron.

MEN OF VIOLENCE BOOKS?!?!

A reader recently contacted me to ask if I was connected with of a line of kindle books under the banner of 'Men of Violence'. I am not connected, but my interest was piqued so I downloaded their four titles, all of which are previously unpublished manuscripts of men's adventure titles which had been commissioned in the 1970s but never printed.

The character names in the e-books have been changed slightly to avoid copyright issues, but **MoV** fanatics will recognise their origins.

The Red-Black Terror by Carter Nicholson = **Nick Carter**

John Falcon Infiltrator #7: The Hollow Earth by Edward Paulsen = **John Eagle: Expeditor**

Super Cop Joe Blitz: The Psycho Killers by Nelson T. Novak = **Super Cop Joe Blaze** with a dose of **Keller/Ryker**

The Triggerman #4: Brains For Brunch by Bruno Scarpetta = **The Marksman/The Sharpshooter**, with the title a nod to the **Gannon** series.

Through a contact I was able to speak with the publisher, who explained the fascinating story as to how they acquired the unpublished manuscripts. They've asked me not to relay the story for fear of recriminations, and insisted that I agree not to reveal their identity.

Of the three MoV books I've read (the **John Falcon** adventure has yet to make it to the top of my to-read pile) all provided a solid slab of 70s style men's adventure fiction. *Brains for Brunch* is very much in the tradition of the later **Marksman** books, typically those carrying a sleazier vibe and gooey sex. *The Psycho Killers* contains recognisable elements of the **Keller** series, especially in terms of the relationship between the abrasive cop and his ex-wife, but is far more outrageous in the sex and violence.

The Red-Black Terror was reminiscent of another Nick Carter book, *The Red Rays*, in which communists use television to brain-wash the American people with porn. Again, it's archetypal of the series, with a globe-trotting plot and a more restrained approach to its purple prose.

It's interesting to me, that despite three different authors penning these books, certain themes and phrases re-occur - sexually aggressive Eurasian women and "jack-hammer thrusts". It undoubtedly reflects the fears of male authors of the time with the rise in women's liberation.

Despite my reservations about how these manuscripts were obtained, they are such glorious trash that I welcome the efforts to make them available and hope more will follow.

11473776R00023

Printed in Great Britain
by Amazon